PRESENT

Rosa
Parks

Ruth Daly

Step 1
Go to www.openlightbox.com

Step 2
Enter this unique code

TDYSASB70

Step 3
Explore your interactive eBook!

AV2 is optimized for use on any device

Your interactive eBook comes with...

Contents
Browse a live contents page to easily navigate through resources

Audio
Listen to sections of the book read aloud

Videos
Watch informative video clips

Weblinks
Gain additional information for research

Slideshows
View images and captions

Try This!
Complete activities and hands-on experiments

Key Words
Study vocabulary, and complete a matching word activity

Quizzes
Test your knowledge

Share
Share titles within your Learning Management System (LMS) or Library Circulation System

Citation
Create bibliographical references following the Chicago Manual of Style

This title is part of our AV2 digital subscription

1-Year K–5 Subscription
ISBN 978-1-7911-3320-7

Access hundreds of AV2 titles with our digital subscription.
Sign up for a FREE trial at **www.openlightbox.com/trial**

Rosa Parks

Contents

Who Was Rosa Parks?

Rosa Parks was an African American **civil rights activist**. In the 1950s, she helped end **racial segregation** in the United States. Rosa took a stand for the rights of all African Americans. She set an example of peaceful protest. Rosa is known as the "mother of the civil rights movement." As such, she is recognized as a symbol of freedom and **equality.**

Rosa was involved in several struggles for civil rights in Alabama. She is best known for refusing to give up her bus seat to a white passenger. After Rosa's bold action on the bus, people organized a bus **boycott**. The Montgomery Bus Boycott led to great changes in civil rights laws.

Rosa became an icon for the civil rights movement. She was awarded a Congressional Gold Medal in 1999. This is the highest honor an American citizen can receive from the U.S. Congress.

Rosa's involvement in civil rights groups helped bring her actions into the spotlight, giving strength to the fight against racial segregation.

Growing Up

Rosa Parks was born Rosa Louise McCauley on February 4, 1913, in Tuskegee, Alabama. She was the eldest of two children. Her father, James, was a carpenter, and her mother, Leona, was a teacher. When Rosa was two years old, her parents separated. She, her brother Sylvester, and their mother moved to Pine Level, Alabama, where Rosa's grandparents had a farm.

Montgomery, established in 1819, was named after General Richard Montgomery, a soldier in the American Revolution. It became the capital of Alabama in 1846.

Rosa spent some of her childhood working on a local **plantation**. At age six, she began picking cotton. When she got older, her job was chopping the cotton. For this work, she earned 50 cents per day. Rosa was homeschooled until she was 11 years old. She then moved to Montgomery, Alabama, to get a better education. Rosa had to leave school before graduating to care for her sick grandmother.

Map of the United States

N
W   E
S

Pacific
Ocean

CANADA

Hawaii

150 miles
150 km

Alaska

500 miles
500 km

UNITED STATES

Alabama

Atlantic
Ocean

SCALE
500 miles
500 kilometers

MEXICO

Gulf of Mexico

LEGEND ■ Alabama ☐ United States ☐ Other Countries
☐ Water ·—·— International Border ·—·— State Border

Alabama Symbols

TREE
Southern
Longleaf Pine

BIRD
Yellowhammer

FLOWER
Camellia

Alabama FACTS

The **population of Alabama** is approximately **5 million.**

Alabama is known for its **timber industry**. Nearly **70 percent** of the state is covered in **trees.**

Alabama is the **30th largest state.** It covers an area of **52,420 square miles** (135,767 sq. km).

Practice Makes Perfect

Strict segregation laws existed in the southern states. **Racism** and violence were common. African Americans were treated as second-class citizens. They could not vote without passing a difficult reading test. Rosa herself failed this test at least two times.

For a short time in the 1940s, Rosa had a job at Maxwell Air Force Base in Montgomery. At Maxwell, some areas were not segregated. Inside the base, African Americans and whites could share public spaces and the transportation system.

While both African American men and women had the right to vote by 1920, many states still prevented them from voting by imposing fees, literacy tests, or threats.

Outside the base, however, things were different. When riding buses, African Americans could only sit in the back section. They had to pay their bus fare at the front. Then, they had to get off the bus and enter again through the rear door. One day in 1943, Rosa refused to exit the bus after paying her fare. The driver, James Blake, shamed Rosa by forcing her off the bus.

In 1943, Rosa joined the National Association for the Advancement of Colored People (NAACP). The NAACP challenged segregation through the court system. Rosa helped African Americans who had been harassed and unjustly accused of crimes. She attended Voters' League meetings, where she learned how to help people sign up to vote. Rosa believed that change could happen if more African Americans voted.

Rosa FACTS

Rosa **returned** to school when she was **19 years old** to complete her **high school education.**

Rosa has written **four books**, including a book she wrote about her life called *Rosa Parks: My Story.*

In Alabama, **December 1st** is known as **Rosa Parks Day.**

The NAACP was founded in 1909 in New York City. By 1919, there were more than 300 branches in cities across the United States.

Key Events

In 1955, Rosa attended a two-week program at the Highlander Folk School in Tennessee. This school focused on the study of workers' rights and the rights of African Americans. The experience proved to Rosa that people could be treated equally in society.

On December 1, 1955, Rosa was going home from her job as a department store seamstress. She boarded a bus and took a seat in the African American section. Soon, there were no seats left for whites. The driver ordered Rosa and three others to move. By coincidence, that driver was James Blake. Three gave up their seats. Rosa refused. Blake called the police, and Rosa was arrested.

During the 1950s, African Americans in Montgomery could not sit in the white section of a bus. The first 10 bus seats were reserved for white passengers.

Thoughts from Rosa

Rosa was committed to equality and fought for it for most of her life. Here are some of the comments she made about the struggle to be treated fairly.

Rosa encouraged people to stand up for what they believe in, even if they are afraid.
"You must never be fearful about what you are doing when it is right."

Rosa talked about the bus boycott.
"The only thing that bothered me was that we waited so long to make this protest."

Rosa discussed her beliefs about the purpose of life for all people.
"I believe we are here on the planet Earth to live, grow up, and do what we can to make this world a better place for all people to enjoy freedom."

Rosa spoke about racism.
"Racism is still with us. But it is up to us to prepare our children for what they have to meet, and, hopefully, we shall overcome."

Rosa was clear on the way she wanted to be remembered.
"I would like to be known as a person who is concerned about freedom and equality and justice and prosperity for all people."

Rosa explained the reason she refused to give up her seat on the bus in 1955.
"People always say that I didn't give up my seat because I was tired, but that isn't true. No, the only tired I was, was tired of giving in."

What Is an Activist?

An activist is someone who works for positive change in society. Activists have strong ideas about society's problems and how to fix them. Their concerns may focus on environmental issues, the unfair treatment of people, or many other things. Activists take action to bring about change. They inform others about causes that are important to them.

RACE LAWS

Race laws, called Jim Crow laws, were common in the South between 1876 and 1963. Southerners passed these laws because they considered whites to be superior to African Americans. Jim Crow laws segregated African Americans in public places such as restaurants, churches, and schools. Rest rooms, elevators, and buses were also segregated. These laws went against the U.S. **Constitution**, which grants full civil rights to all.

Activists bring awareness to important issues by organizing and attending marches. They hold protests and large meetings to bring attention to their cause. They meet with politicians and other leaders to try to change laws. Activists often represent people who cannot speak for themselves. Rosa Parks is known as a civil rights activist because she challenged the race laws in Alabama. By doing this, she tried to make society better for everyone, regardless of their skin color.

Activists 101

Yelena Bonner
(1923–2011)

Yelena Bonner was a nurse and later a doctor in the former **Soviet Union**. She became active in civil rights in the late 1960s, along with her husband, physicist Andrei Sakharov. Both spent time **exiled** in the Soviet city of Gorky. Their crime was criticizing the government. Yelena worked tirelessly to help those being treated unjustly. She spent her life speaking out for the **oppressed** people of her homeland.

Coretta Scott King
(1927–2006)

Coretta Scott King worked alongside her husband, the Reverend Dr. Martin Luther King, Jr., on civil rights issues. She joined the Montgomery Bus Boycott. She also worked to bring about a law called the Civil Rights Act. After the **assassination** of her husband, Coretta founded the Martin Luther King, Jr. Center for Nonviolent Social Change in Atlanta, Georgia. She traveled the world speaking about equal rights for all people.

Ibrahim Rugova
(1944–2006)

Ibrahim Rugova was a college professor and writer from the former Serbian province of Kosovo. In the late 1980s, the Serbian government took away the rights of Kosovo's Albanian citizens. Ibrahim used peaceful means to help make Kosovo free and fair for all. He was elected Kosovo's new president in 2002, but died before Kosovo became free.

Shirin Ebadi
(1947–)

Shirin Ebadi, a lawyer, became Iran's first female judge in 1969. She lost that position in 1979, after the Islamic Revolution. In 2001, she co-founded the Defenders of Human Rights Center, which defends Iranians against unjust government actions. In 2003, Shirin was awarded the Nobel Peace Prize. Today, she is Iran's most widely known human rights activist.

Influences

Marcus Garvey

From an early age, Rosa was influenced by her maternal grandfather, Sylvester Edwards. Edwards was a former slave. He had seen firsthand the violent acts of the **Ku Klux Klan** against African Americans. Klansmen would stop at nothing, including murder, to control African Americans through fear.

Rosa attended Montgomery's St. Paul African Methodist Episcopal Church in Montgomery. She also taught Sunday school there.

Edwards was a supporter of Marcus Garvey. Garvey was a political leader who encouraged African Americans to take pride in their racial heritage. Edwards passed on this sense of pride to his granddaughter. Rosa never accepted the idea that being an African American made her inferior to white people.

Another influence in Rosa's life was the African Methodist Episcopal church. Rosa attended the church from childhood and developed a strong Christian faith. Her faith proved to be a source of strength when she was harassed and threatened. Rosa stated that she felt sorry for the people who threw rocks at her and called her names.

THE PARKS FAMILY

In December 1932, Rosa McCauley married Raymond Parks. Raymond was a successful Montgomery barber. He was also a respected member of the African American community there. Raymond encouraged Rosa to finish high school and get her diploma. She finally did so in 1934.

Rosa and Raymond shared a belief that all people deserved equal rights. Both belonged to the powerful NAACP. Raymond helped raise money to provide lawyers for young African American men unfairly accused of crimes. The Parks had no children of their own. However, they made a point of helping many young African Americans.

Overcoming Obstacles

Following her arrest, Rosa was charged with breaking the segregation law. She was fined a total of $14. News of her arrest soon spread through the African American community. In response, civil rights leaders set up a boycott of Montgomery's buses. The next day, thousands of African Americans walked, carpooled, or shared taxis to get to work.

The Montgomery Bus Boycott lasted for 381 days. One of the leaders of the boycott was Martin Luther King, Jr. Dozens of the boycott leaders were arrested. Rosa appealed her own arrest. She argued that the law under which she was charged was illegal.

During the bus boycott, many people in the white community were angry with Rosa and other civil rights leaders. African Americans were attacked and arrested. Their churches were burned down, and many homes were firebombed.

The Montgomery Improvement Association was created to organize the bus boycott. Martin Luther King, Jr. was chosen as the group's president.

The boycott caused problems for Rosa and Raymond as well. In January 1956, Rosa lost her job at the department store. Not allowed to even talk to his coworkers about the bus incident, Raymond quit his job. The Parks' landlord raised their rent, and they were unable to find new jobs. They experienced continual threats and **discrimination.** Finally, in 1957, the couple moved to Detroit, Michigan, to live near Rosa's brother and his family.

In 2003, the restored bus Rosa was riding in 1955 debuted in the "Celebrate Black History" program at the Henry Ford Museum in Dearborn, Michigan.

Achievements and Successes

In December 1956, one year after the bus incident, the Supreme Court of the United States made an important ruling. It became illegal to limit African Americans to certain sections of public buses. However, it was not until 1964 that things really changed. That year, the Civil Rights Act made racial discrimination illegal in all public places.

Rosa returned to Alabama many times to attend civil rights meetings. In 1965, she joined Martin Luther King, Jr. and thousands of others in a civil rights march to Montgomery. The marchers demanded equal voting rights for all. Later that year, President Lyndon Johnson signed the Voting Rights Act. This law made it easier for African Americans to vote.

In 2019, a statue of Rosa Parks was unveiled in Montgomery, Alabama, to celebrate the 64th anniversary of Rosa's refusal to give up her bus seat.

Rosa received countless honors and awards for her lifelong civil rights work. Among these many awards were the Presidential Medal of Freedom. She was admitted to the International Women's Forum International Hall of Fame in 1998. In 1999, *Time* magazine named Rosa one of the 20th century's most influential people.

Rosa died on October 24, 2005, at her home in Detroit. She was 92 years old. Rosa became the first African American woman to have her body lay in state in the U.S. Capitol Rotunda in Washington, DC. In February 2013, on the 100th anniversary of Rosa's' birth, the U.S. Postal Service released the "Rosa Parks Forever" stamp in her honor.

HELPING OTHERS

In 1987, Rosa co-founded the Rosa and Raymond Parks Institute for Self Development with her friend Elaine Eason Steele. This organization helps Detroit's African American youth find jobs. It also educates them about African American history. The institute's "Pathways to Freedom" bus tours take young people to many important civil rights sites.

Write a Biography

A person's life story can be the subject of a book. This kind of book is called a biography. Biographies describe the lives of remarkable people, such as those who have achieved great success or have taken important actions to help others. These people may be alive today, or they may have lived many years ago. Reading a biography can help you learn more about a remarkable person.

At school, you might be asked to write a biography. First, decide who you want to write about. You can choose an activist, such as Rosa Parks, or any other person. Then, find out if your library has any resources about this person. Learn as much as you can about him or her. Write down the key events in this person's life. What was this person's childhood like? What has he or she accomplished? What are his or her goals? What makes this person special or unusual?

A concept web is a useful research tool. Read the questions in the following concept web. Answer the questions in your notebook. Your answers will help you write a biography.

Adulthood

- Where does this individual currently reside?
- Does he or she have a family?

Childhood

- Where and when was this person born?
- Describe his or her parents, siblings, and friends.
- Did this person grow up in unusual circumstances?

Your Opinion

- What did you learn from your research?
- Would you suggest these books to others?
- Was anything missing from these books?

Writing a Biography

Work and Preparation

- What was this person's education?
- What was his or her work experience?
- How does this person work? What is or was the process he or she uses or used?

Main Accomplishments

- What is this person's life's work?
- Has he or she received awards or recognition for accomplishments?
- How have this person's accomplishments served others?

Help and Obstacles

- Did this individual have a positive attitude?
- Did he or she receive help from others?
- Did this person have a mentor?
- Did this person face any hardships? If so, how were the hardships overcome?

Rosa Parks Timeline

Rosa Parks Events		World Events During
Rosa Louise McCauley is born on February 4, 1913.	1913	The First Balkan War ends in Europe.
Rosa marries Raymond Parks on December 18.	1932	Amelia Earhart becomes the first woman to fly solo across the Atlantic Ocean.
Rosa is forced to leave a bus for refusing to exit and re-enter using the rear door.	1943	During World War II, Jews in Warsaw, Poland, rebel against the Nazis.
Rosa is arrested and charged for refusing to give up her seat on a bus, and the Montgomery Bus Boycott begins.	1955	Singer Elvis Presley makes his first appearance on television.
The Rosa and Raymond Parks Institute for Self Development is co-founded by Rosa.	1987	Margaret Thatcher is re-elected prime minister of the United Kingdom.
Rosa Parks dies on October 24.	2005	NASA grounds the Space Shuttle program.
President Joe Biden redecorates the Oval Office to honor historical figures. Additions include a sculpture of Rosa Parks.	2021	Juneteenth, the day that marks the end of slavery in the United States, officially becomes a federal holiday.

Key Words

assassination: the murder of a person for political reasons

boycott: to stop using something as a way to object

civil rights activist: someone who fights for people's basic rights to freedom and equal treatment

constitution: a group of written laws that explain how a country is governed

discrimination: treating someone unfairly based on his or her race, gender, age, or abilities

equality: fair treatment for all people

exiled: forced to leave someplace

Ku Klux Klan: a secret society that believes that white people are superior to other races

oppressed: unwillingly controlled and held down by those in power

plantation: a farm, especially in a hot part of the world, where crops are grown

racial segregation: the keeping apart of people from different racial groups

racism: being against a race of people due to believing they are not as good as one's own race

Soviet Union: a country formerly located in eastern Europe and northwestern Asia

Index

Get the best of both worlds.

AV2 bridges the gap between print and digital.

The expandable resources toolbar enables quick access to content including **videos**, **audio**, **activities**, **weblinks**, **slideshows**, **quizzes**, and **key words**.

Animated videos make static images come alive.

Resource icons on each page help readers to further **explore key concepts**.

Published by Lightbox Learning Inc.
276 5th Avenue
Suite 704 #917
New York, NY 10001
Website: www.openlightbox.com

Library of Congress Cataloging-in-Publication Data
Names: Daly, Ruth, 1962- author.
Title: Rosa Parks / Ruth Daly.
Description: New York, NY : Lightbox Learning Inc., [2023] | Series: History makers : past and present | Includes index. |
   Audience: Grades 4-6
Identifiers: LCCN 2022001790 (print) | LCCN 2022001791 (ebook) | ISBN 9781791146375 (library binding) |
   ISBN 9781791146382 (paperback) | ISBN 9781791146399
Subjects: LCSH: Parks, Rosa, 1913-2005--Juvenile literature. | African American women civil rights workers--Alabama--
   Montgomery--Biography--Juvenile literature. | African American civil rights workers--Alabama--Montgomery--
   Biography--Juvenile literature. | Civil rights workers--Alabama--Montgomery--Biography--Juvenile literature. |
   Segregation in transportation--Alabama--Montgomery--History--20th century--Juvenile literature. | Montgomery (Ala.)--
   Social conditions--20th century--Juvenile literature.
Classification: LCC F334.M753 P3733 2023 (print) | LCC F334.M753 (ebook) | DDC 323.092 [B]--dc23/eng/20220131
LC record available at https://lccn.loc.gov/2022001790
LC ebook record available at https://lccn.loc.gov/2022001791

Printed in Guangzhou, China
1 2 3 4 5 6 7 8 9 0 26 25 24 23 22

022022
101121

Project Coordinator: Heather Kissock
Designer: Terry Paulhus

Photo Credits
Every reasonable effort has been made to trace ownership and to obtain permission to reprint copyright material. The publisher would be pleased to have any errors or omissions brought to its attention so that they may be corrected in subsequent printings. The publisher acknowledges Alamy, Getty Images, and Shutterstock as its primary image suppliers for this title.